Capture Your Vision

The Nehemiah Principles

A Manual for Leaders

Lorraine E. Thomas, M.Ed.

For information regarding permission to use content from this material, write to Life Empowering Truths, P.O. Box 801479 Acworth, GA 30101

Capture Your Vision: The Nehemiah Principles Manual is a workbook designed to help visionaries capture what they have seen in their mind's eye and make it plain in the natural realm where others can see it / by Lorraine E. Thomas.

Editing: Mary Herrygers

Table of Contents

"Write the vision and make it plain on tablets, that he may run who reads it." -Habakkuk 2:2

About the Manual

Included in this manual are guided questions to help you bring your dreams to fruition. Use the successful strategies that Nehemiah used to rebuild the walls in Jerusalem.

Background

The principles in the manual are taken from the book of Nehemiah. The man - Nehemiah was one of many Jews who had been taken captive during the Persian Empire. We know little about his life prior to his becoming cupbearer to the king of Persia (Nehemiah 1:1). A cup-bearer was an officer of high rank, whose duty it was to serve the drinks at the king's table. Due to the constant fear of plots and conspiracies, a person had to be regarded as thoroughly trustworthy to hold this position. Nehemiah served faithfully in his position as an officer in the royal courts of King Artaxerxes. The role came with risks, yet it gave him full access to the ruler of the land. Nevertheless, it is important to remember that Nehemiah was still a slave.

Nehemiah's Passion

Nehemiah was greatly distressed when he was told that the remnant of Jews who escaped exile were in great trouble. They were living in deplorable conditions and they were at the mercies of their enemies. The wall of Jerusalem was broken down and the gates had been destroyed by fire. Nehemiah's passion became clear after he received the news. (Nehemiah 1:4) The Bible says that after he heard the news he sat down and wept and mourned for days. Not only that, he fasted and prayed constantly. He recognized a need for deliverance and he didn't turn away from it. He connected his passion to his purpose. The way he organized the rebuilding of the wall of Jerusalem is a great example of true leadership.

Nehemiah's Leadership Principles

Nehemiah started out with a passion to help his people, but he would not have been successful without a plan of action. In this manual, you will find seven principles of leadership that worked to bring his vision to pass. These ideologies will help you prepare for the process of bringing what you have seen in the unseen into visible manifestation. Without a plan, you will ultimately fail.

In addition, do not expect to do great things in the future if you fail to do small things in a great way now. See yourself as a leader and begin to bloom where you are planted. True leaders:

Live a life that is worth emulating
Equip themselves with the necessary tools and information to be effective
Ask for help (Pray and seek out mentors)
Don't quit

Leadership Principle #1

Connect Your Passion to Your Purpose

Your vision may begin with a concern about the ruins. The ruins represent the problem that you need to solve and the people you are called to help. You will never be a great leader until you first become concerned about the needs and concerns of those around you.

Ultimately, your purpose in life will always lead you to help others. By serving others, you serve God. What moves your heart? If you are being guided by a strong desire to do a certain thing and you can't seem to move away from it, do not ignore that desire. It may not be something radical, but it will be something that will allow you to leave your mark on the world. Causes that burden you normally move you to take action. The thing that you are most passionate about is usually a good indication of what you were created to do. Your passion is connected to certain gifts, talents and abilities that make you uniquely *you*.

Your Gift is Valuable

It is very easy to believe that the work you do in a church is the only way to serve others. This is not true. Any legitimate work can be used by God to benefit mankind and bring glory to His name. Do not devalue honest work deemed as secular if the work that you do is meeting a need in the life of someone else. Parenthood, caregivers and firefighters are all perfect examples of vocations that serve and impact the life of others. Rick Warren says in The Purpose Driven Life, "Work becomes worship when you dedicate it to God and perform it with an awareness of His presence."[1]

Author's Notes

Nearly ten years ago, I was given a vision to start a mentor and leadership program for teens and a similar training organization for women. The programs would restore foundational values essential for wellbeing **and** *bring emotional healing to women. At*

---

[1] Rick Warren, The Purpose Driven Life. Grand Rapids: Zondervan, 2002. p. 67.

first, I was very hesitant about the dream even though I had been a classroom teacher for a number of years, served as a Sunday school teacher, a counselor at a crisis pregnancy center, youth leader and had been asked to speak at various functions in churches and schools. In spite of those experiences, fear would not allow me to tell anyone about the vision, not even my husband.

Years before the vision was given to me, I remember being very concerned about youngsters who lacked respect for authority. I was also perturbed and dismayed about the destructive practices in our society that were eroding family values and devaluing humanity. I did not feel qualified or prepared to take on such a task, so I tucked the vision away on a shelf in my mind and continued to move forward with my plans in becoming a school principal. I enrolled in an Administration and Supervision course at the University of Georgia to pursue my dreams; not knowing that my previous experiences and education were preparing me for my current role as founder and president of a nonprofit organization.

Months after the dream was given to me, my husband and I were traveling home from a trip to Virginia. As we neared our house, he pointed to a building and told me he thought it would be a nice place for me to have a program to work with kids. Needless to say, I was speechless because I had not shared the vision with him. Not long after that incident, I attended a funeral for a co-worker's son and encountered an older women who told me that God wanted her to tell me that I was supposed to work with teens and women. That was my burning bush experience. Once again, I was dumbstruck. A few months later, I stepped out in faith and began Destiny's Daughters of Promise, a mentor and leadership program for teen girls. It is now years later and we have served hundreds of girls.

I cannot tell you that the process was easy. It challenged me in ways I never would have imagined. I jokingly say to people that if I had known all that would be required and the sacrifices that would be made to move forward with the vision, I would have run the other way.

Your experience may not be like mine. It may as simple as Nehemiah's. He was burdened with a desire to help his countrymen. Know that your divine purpose, ministry, assignment or call will impact your life and the life of others for good. It will never be just about you. Instead, your unique talents and abilities will be used for the betterment of mankind.

Did you know that you can only walk in courage in the face of fear? Do not be afraid to step out in faith.

Below, describe what you are most passionate about.

_____

_____

_____

_____

_____

_____

_____

_____

_____

Leadership Principle #2

Know Your Target Audience

Who will you help? You have to know who your target audience is in order to meet their needs. If you are unsure, take a look around and assess the situations and needs around you. If you are moved to take action about a particular wrong, disaster, human suffering or societal ill, think about who would benefit from a solution.

As stated previously, Nehemiah had a burden for his countrymen in Jerusalem. The Jews needed hope, provisions, security and most importantly, they needed to reconnect with God. Nehemiah prayed and interceded for them. God gave him this passion for the people because He wanted Nehemiah to help them.

Author's Notes

As stated earlier, I was given a vision to work with teens and women. With so many needs in the world today, it would be very easy to turn my attention to other pressing issues. I am moved by certain injustices, political and economic issues in our nation. Even though it would not be a bad thing to become an advocate for those suffering as a result, my focus has to remain on my target audience. I can continue to pray and provide assistance for certain needs as they arise, but I cannot allow myself to become so involved in working to solve those issues that I lose sight of the assignment given to me.

It is more important for me to remember my mission and those I serve; trusting that God has appointed others to work on other societal problems.

Answer the following questions to help you identify your target population.

1. Is your passion for men, women or children? Refer back to the vision or dream that you were given and try to be as specific as possible.

   _____

2. Are you passionate about helping the homeless, the abused, orphans, the elderly, children, addicts, prostitutes or the poor? It may be that you have a burden to help

immigrants, veterans, persecuted groups, incarcerated individuals or the illiterate. (Be specific).

_____

3. What types of agencies are already providing help to your target group?

_____

_____

Leadership Principle #3

Unpack the Vision and Make it Plain

Before you can effectively solve a problem, you need a clear understanding of what the problem is and what has to be done to solve it. In the first chapter of Nehemiah, he prayed about the problem after he heard the reports from his relatives. He believed that the people needed protection from their enemy; which is why he wanted to rebuild the walls. Nehemiah had access to fine wine and other delicacies, but he didn't ask for those things to take to the people. He specifically asked the king for permission to cut down trees for the timber needed to rebuild the gates and walls of the city.

Take the time to get firsthand knowledge about the needs you plan to address. By properly assessing the situation, you will have a better idea of the services you need to provide. After Nehemiah arrived in Jerusalem, he assessed the damages for himself. Prior to coming, he only had secondhand information. Understand that you will need to go beyond reports gathered on a computer or what you read in books. When you set out to help people, they will connect with you a lot quicker when they know that you have a handle on their situation.

Share the vision after you are clear about the state of affairs. Nehemiah was more effective as a leader because he verified the situation before addressing it publicly with the people. He gathered his facts. You will need to convince others of the importance of the problem you plan to address.

Author's Notes

As an educator, I was aware of many of the problems my students and parents faced. I remember the day that one of my students confided in me that she hated her father. The pain that she carried within ran deep.

On this particular day, I had taken the class out for recess and took note of the fact that one of my students seemed aloof and had little interaction with the other students. When I asked her why she seemed so sad and depressed, she began to tell me about her dad.

"Mrs. Thomas, I hate my dad!"

She was upset by the fact that her sister's father came to see her often and did things with her. Her tone conveyed the resentment and sadness in her soul. She explained that her father never did anything with her and he always made promises that he did not keep.

It was hard to address this emotional hurt during the school day, but it was an issue that was impacting the wellbeing of this child. Years later, this little girl would be one of the first students to join Destiny's Daughters of Promise. One of the seven key areas of the program is relationship building techniques. Because of that encounter with her, I had firsthand knowledge of some of the struggles she faced.

Circle the method that is best suited to your purpose for collecting information about the problem.

Surveys/Questionnaires   Focus groups/Public forums

The two main ways of gathering information include: quantitative and qualitative methods. Quantitative reveal results in numbers. You will learn how many, how much or how often. Qualitative yield results by allowing you to observe interactions or do interviews.

Surveys can be used to attain quantitative data. You can gain information from your target audience in a written format, face to face or by telephone.

Focus groups and public forums can provide qualitative information. Qualitative information will help you gather information that is not easily measured or translated into numbers. They provide information behind the numbers. For example, you will learn the feelings or the history behind the response.

What resources, provisions or services will you provide?

_____

_____

If you will be providing services, are you qualified to deliver it? _____

If not, do you have connections with those who can provide the needed services? _____

Leadership Principle #4

Develop a Solid Plan of Action

Nehemiah committed himself to a plan of action after spending much time in prayer. He didn't rush out immediately to tackle the problem. After he inquired about the Jewish exiles, he prayed.

> *"So it was, when I heard these words that I sat down and wept, and mourned for many days; I was fasting and praying before the God of heaven."*- Nehemiah 1:4

It was during this time of prayer and fasting that God gave him a strategy. Nehemiah stated that he told no one what God had put in his heart to do at Jerusalem. Nehemiah 2:11.

When Nehemiah was given the opportunity to speak to the king about the troubles of his countrymen, he already had an idea of what he wanted to do. He was able to tell the king how long he would be gone. He knew that he needed a letter that would allow him safe passage through the region and he asked for trees from the king's forest to make beams for the gates. Nehemiah didn't come up with a plan of action on the spot, he had spent time in prayer as he thought about the situation. The king not only granted his request, he also volunteered to send captains of the army and horsemen as an escort. God was answering Nehemiah's prayer to move in the king's heart.

Author's Notes

Seek out mentors who will not be threatened by your success. These mentors can help you clearly define your vision. They may share valuable information that will help you hone in on key elements that will impact the vision.

Before I began Destiny's Daughters of Promise, I met with school board members, principals and other community leaders involved in similar organizations and shared my vision for the program. They gave me ideas and shared some insights that proved to be invaluable to me. It was in my best interest to get the help and advice of others. I had never started an organization before, so I did not know where to start. Their feedback helped me to put a business plan together and it also allowed me the opportunity to plan for things that I had not considered. I would also advise you to pray and ask for God's leading and direction before sharing your vision with others. Everyone will not be happy for you and there will those who will work to stop you.

Be sure to get answers to these questions before launching the vision:

What resources will you need to solve the problem?

_____

_____

_____

_____

Where will you provide the services?

_____

_____

_____

If you need a building, will you buy, rent or seek use of donated space?

_____

How will you generate the income you need to pay for the resources, supplies, building etc.?

_____

_____

_____

_____

_____

Nehemiah gave the people an opportunity to be involved in the solution by allowing them to work in the rebuilding of the wall. The people had a personal investment in the success of the project. They knew that the wall would provide protection to keep their family safe.

On the lines below, write how you will get those you help involved in the process.

_____

_____

_____

_____

_____

Leadership Principle #5

Know Your Strengths

Did you know that you are the answer to a problem? God, in His infinite wisdom created you for a specific purpose. The question is, what problem were you created to solve? Medical doctors provide care for the sick. Politicians serve as representatives to govern and address issues that affect citizens in the community. These positions are the answers to a particular problem.

After Nehemiah prayed about the problem, he committed to doing something about it. He realized that the people were in a vulnerable state. They needed provisions and protection. Only after he set out to solve the problem was he given an opportunity to demonstrate the leadership skills and abilities that were already inside of him.

Seize opportunities

The problems you face are really opportunities for you to show what you can do. Nelson Mandela's imprisonment didn't break him; it strengthened him. It was the platform used to reveal the true leader that he was. His prison cell served as the launching pad that propelled him to the presidency.

> *"Then I said to them, "You see the distress that we are in, how Jerusalem lies waste, and its gates are burned with fire. Come and let us build the wall of Jerusalem, that we may no longer be a reproach." 18 And I told them of the hand of my God which had been good upon me, and also of the king's words that he had spoken to me. So they said, "Let us rise up and build." Then they set their hands to this good work."*- Nehemiah 2:17-18

Nehemiah gave the people a reason to believe in him. Credible leaders attract passionate and committed followers, and people want to join them in their efforts. Nehemiah told the people what he planned to do and he explained that God had given him this assignment. He also assured them that he had the backing of the king. This statement reassured the people that he had the ability to lead this effort. We all have something of value. What do you have to offer those in need?

Nehemiah had the ability to make an impact because of his strengths. He had great organizational and administrative skills. Nehemiah was also courageous, empathetic, decisive and a man of deep spiritual conviction. His passion to help his people compelled him to make an impact that brought about lasting change.

Leaders who get things done, stand on strong building blocks of leadership. On the lines below, write down the skills you possess.

_____

_____

_____

_____

_____

Placing emphasis on your credibility allows your followers to view you as a reliable leader and it is one way to gain the respect of those you lead. Your education, experiences or connections may help to prove your reliability as a leader. When people believe that they can trust you to handle a situation it will translate into improved performance under your leadership. It is important to note that when God calls you to do a specific work, He has already equipped you with everything you need to be successful. A part of the process may include finding ways to develop your gifts and talents.

> *But to each one of us grace was given according to the measure of Christ's gift."*-Ephesians 4:7

Paul told Timothy that he needed to stir up the gift of God that was already inside him. Specifically, he told Timothy that he needed to study to show himself approved. Whatever your gift is, you will have to develop it through study and work.

What previous experience, education or knowledge have you had to prepare you to lead in this effort?

_____

_____

_____

Author's Notes

Although I had experience working with youth and had served in leadership roles, I felt inadequate to lead. I questioned my actions at every turn. I respected the opinions of others whom I felt had more leadership skills and knowledge more than my own. I had many sleepless nights because I kept second guessing myself.

I began reading books on effective leadership principles and spent time investing in the materials of leaders I respected. In addition, I came to the realization that I had not given myself the vision. I believe that it was a vision given to me by God and He knew what my skills and talents were before He chose me. I gave the insecurities to Him and began to remind myself of my previous leadership experiences. It helped to remind myself why I was serving and how beneficial the program was for those I was helping.

As you move forward with your vision you may miss it every now and then, but you can learn from every mistake. Choose to focus on the things you do well and forgive yourself for the momentary lapses.

Leadership Principle #6

Organize the Right Team

Any great work will always require the support of a group of committed people. If you can complete the task alone, chances are you are working on a personal project. Your greatest impact will require outreach and in order to do that, you will need the help of others.

Nehemiah put a team in place quickly, but he organized them well. He excelled in this task because:

1. **He was clear about the vision** and he articulated it well to the team members. He told them what the problem was, what he was prepared to do and how they could help.

2. **He set SMART goals** – Nehemiah had a strategy to reach the desired goal. You may need to consult with others who can help you. Setting clear goals will give you an idea of what success will look like.

3. **He led the efforts** – Nehemiah risked his life, stepped out of his comfort zone and he tapped into his own resources to make the dream a reality. If you are not going to invest in your vision why should others?

4. **He chose helpers based on their gifts, talents and abilities** – Look beyond external factors when choosing your team. Consider how well the individuals you are considering perform now. Do they follow through on their commitments? Are they team players? Do they verbally bash leaders? Do they follow well?

5. **He kept the team on track** – You will have to keep your team moving toward the vision. Things will begin to fall apart when you allow people and situations to cause you to lose sight of the vision. Ignoring distractions will be difficult, but you actually serve as an inspiration for the team when they see progress.

Nehemiah 4:6 says the people had a heart to work when they saw progress being made.

6. **He ignored the attempts of the enemy to divert his attention from the work** – As a leader, you will need to watch for traps that can derail the vision. Nehemiah's enemies were crafty in their efforts to hinder the progress of the work. They lied, threatened and secretly planned an attack against the project, but they all failed. Stay focused!

7. **He dealt with internal problems appropriately** – Nehemiah listened when the people came to him with their problems as described in Nehemiah 5. He took time to reflect on the concerns before responding. His actions required a great deal of courage because he had to confront others about their wickedness. Ignoring the situation could have ruined all of the efforts that had gone into the work. His ability to listen to the people showed that he cared about them and valued them. Nehemiah relied on the wisdom of God to handle both external and internal conflicts that could have ended the work.

Author's Notes

Unlike Nehemiah, it took me quite some time to develop the skills needed to manage difficult people. I preferred to avoid confrontations and when I did confront, the outcome usually led to a parting of ways. One important lesson I had to learn was to respond and not react to negative behaviors. When you respond, you do so from a place of strength. A reaction is normally the result of weakness. If someone is able to make you act in a manner inconsistent with who you are because anger has overtaken you, it shows that you need to work on self-control.

Do not allow your emotions to be controlled or manipulated by someone who will make you say and do things that you will later regret. By choosing when and how you respond to people will increase your self-confidence because you can be assured about your motives and decision-making.

In addition, I had to learn to examine the impact of my own behaviors and attitudes to determine if it contributed to the situation. After careful consideration, I now pray for wisdom to know how to respond effectively. Of course, there may still be times when the best solution is to part ways. Most importantly, do not shy away from difficult people. Left unchallenged, they will undermine your efforts.

Leadership Principle #7

Lead With Humility

Nehemiah had the right perspectives about himself and what he was called to do. He began his vision with a pure heart. He wanted to help others. He knew that he was not able to do it without the help of God. He spent time in prayer to petition the Lord on behalf of the people and he also took the time that was needed to wait on God for a plan. After the completion of the wall, it would have been very easy for Nehemiah to be lifted up in pride over his accomplishments. Instead, he turned over the control of the city to someone else. He didn't get it twisted. The assignment was to build the wall and return to his position as cupbearer. It would have been very easy for him to get caught up in pride and go beyond the assignment he was given. After all, he got the process started, risked his life and made himself uncomfortable for the people's sake.

Nehemiah did not try to put all of the focus on himself. He was a man of humility. When the work was done, he immediately brought in Ezra, the priest to encourage the people to turn their hearts to God.

> *"Thus I purified them from everything foreign and appointed duties for the priests and the Levites, each in his task, 31 and I arranged for the supply of wood at appointed times and for the first fruits. Remember me, O my God, for good."*- Nehemiah 13:30-31

Eventually, Nehemiah was made governor of Jerusalem. Undoubtedly, it was because he remained a man committed to the plans and purposes of God from beginning to end.

Author's Notes

I have been told that the most important test will come when you reach your goal and you are successful. It is important for me to remind myself that it is God's grace that I am allowed to do what I am doing. It may sound like a cliché, but I honestly cannot take any credit for any level of success. With all of my mess ups and hang ups, things really should not be going as well as they are. I have had the help and support of many on this journey. Some were with me for only a season, but they left something behind that served to make my job easier in some way or an experience that taught me how to recognize situations that I needed to avoid at all cost.

Final Thoughts

Operate in Excellence

Strive to be a person of excellence and integrity in things that you do. Even though Nehemiah held a prominent position in the king's court, he was not a free man. Think about that. The life of a slave was a lowly position, but Nehemiah obviously excelled in small things before he was promoted to serve in such a prestigious position. I cannot emphasize enough how important it is for you to start small. Do not despise the day of small beginnings.

As you work towards your goal, do not become discouraged by others who are doing it bigger and better. The only time that you will ever start out on top is when you are digging a hole. Cultivating a seed will take time and it is in your best interest not to rush it. Take the time that is necessary to build a good foundation. You will need more time than you think to learn and grow through the process of bringing your vision to a level of fruitfulness.

Write your mission statement, vision and values using the sample below.

SAMPLE

Good Neighbor's House

Mission:

Good Neighbor's House provides food, shelter and training services to eliminate homelessness in Metro Atlanta.

Vision:

Good Neighbor's House is known as a premier community resource center for the homeless. We provide a unique blend of outreach and education to the homeless enabling them to become contributing members of society.

Our Values:

Good Neighbor's House is committed to serving in professional excellence and providing personal attention to our homeless population. We offer our clients the opportunity to learn and develop in a safe and enriching environment.

Using the information you wrote as you answered the questions in the manual, write your mission, vision and values statement.

Your mission statement:

Your vision:

Your values:

Make the Vision Plain

It is time to write the vision. Use the sample vision outline below to create your vision.

Vision Outline

    I.   Identify your vision

           A. What is your passion

           B. How can you connect your passion to your purpose

    II.   Write the vision

           A. Who will you help

           B. What services will you provide

           C. What resources will you need

           D. How will things be better because of the services you provide

    III.   Create a plan of action

           A. When will you begin

           B. What results will you have after 3, 5, 10 years

           C. How will you achieve the goal?

           D. How will you know that the mission is a success

To create a plan of action, you will need to set goals. To do this, break the vision down into smaller parts that are measurable.

*This outline is not a business or strategic plan, but it can be used to help you work through the steps in writing out those plans.

ABOUT THE AUTHOR

For nearly 20 years, Lorraine has been assisting others in finding ways to achieve their goals. She builds upon her experience as an educator and instructional coach to conduct training and workshop sessions to adults and teens. She has experience speaking to diverse audiences on topics ranging from basic life skills and leadership to relationship issues. Most notably, she is the founder of Destiny's Daughters of Promise and Life Empowering Truths – a ministry providing learning experiences for women to help them discover their gifts, talents and abilities and increase their knowledge of the Word of God.

Lorraine has a master's degree in Education and is certified in Supervision and Administration. She resides in the Metro Atlanta area with her husband, Charles. They have been married nearly thirty years. Lorraine is active in her local church where she serves in the Ministry of Christian Education.

Books by Lorraine Thomas

Unequally Yoked

A Promise to Love

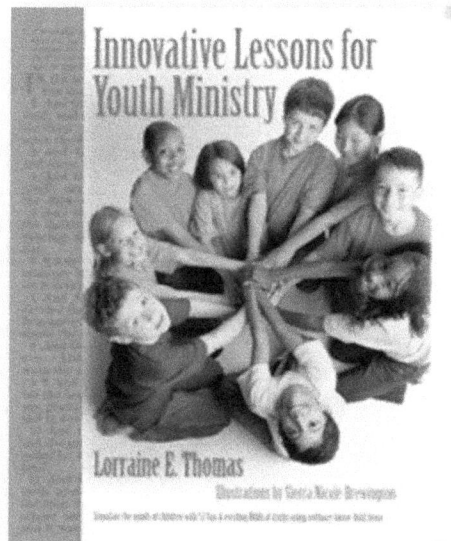

Innovative Lessons for Youth Ministry

Connect with us

Connect with us on Facebook, LinkedIn, and Twitter or visit us on the web at www.lorrainethomas.com. If this manual has been a help to you, please connect with us and share your comments.

To book Lorraine for your event, please complete the information below and send your request to:

Life Empowering Truths
P.O. Box 801479
Acworth, GA 30101

Name (Please print)

_____

Description of your event:

_____

_____

_____

Date of Event:

Contact Number:

Email Address:

I would like Lorraine to serve as a:

Keynote Speaker   Conference host   Workshop facilitator   Trainer

www.ingramcontent.com/pod-product-compliance
Lightning Source LLC
Chambersburg PA
CBHW081234020426
42331CB00012B/3176